THE MOST IMPORTANT DECISION

STARTING THE JOURNEY OF FAITH

BY

ROGER D. HABER

Published by GreatCloud publications

ISBN-13: 978-1985410411
ISBN-10: 1985410419

Scripture quotations are taken from the Holy Bible, New Living Translation, copyright ©1996, 2004, 2015 by Tyndale House Foundation. Used by permission of Tyndale House Publishers, Inc., Carol Stream, Illinois 60188. All rights reserved.

Book Cover Design: germancreative

DEDICATION

to

Our Church Family

First Baptist Church
Randolph, MA

ALSO BY ROGER D. HABER

- *Christmas First Persons—Sharing the Story Creatively*
- *Do All Dogs Go to Heaven?—Grieving the Loss of Your Pet*
- *You Better Learn Baby Talk! You're a Grandparent!*

COMING SOON—

- *A Great Cloud of Witnesses—Listening to Faith Heroes*
- *The Church as Orchestra—A Symphony of Praise to the Master Composer*
- *Unwrapping God's Christmas Gift*
- *Praying as Jesus Prayed—Reflections from the Lord's Prayer*

ACKNOWLEDGEMENTS

Nanci Haber, editor

The Most Important Decision
Starting the Journey of Faith

Introduction

Whatʼs the most important decision youʼve ever made?

Take your time. You probably have to think about it.

Over the next few pages, Iʼd like to suggest to you that there is a **most important decision**. We make lots of decisions every day. But there is a **most important decision**.

Do you know what that is?

Keep reading.

There are some decisions that are basically inconsequential. What kind of cereal you have for breakfast, what color socks you wear tomorrow,

THE MOST IMPORTANT DECISION

or whether you part your hair on the right, left or middle really doesn't affect your life all that much.

But the **most important decision** you might make after reading this book will have a profound impact on your life from this day forward—and for all eternity.

I'll remind you of this at the end too—but if you make this **most important decision**, would you let me know?

Thanks.

Just email me at roger@rogerhaber.com.

Chapter 1
Decisions, Decisions

Decisions, decisions. We make them every day and throughout the day.

What time will I get up? What will I have for breakfast? Captain Crunch or Oatmeal?

Should I go to the gym? Which route will I take to work or school?

What will I wear today? Business casual or the jeans?

Then there are decisions which are higher on the decision making scale:

Should I get married? And to whom?

Should we have children? How many?

THE MOST IMPORTANT DECISION

Which school should I attend? Harvard or the Community College?

Which job should I apply for?

These are all important decisions—but not the **most important decision**.

The **most important decision** a person can make will change that person's life forever—and for all eternity.

Are you interested in reading on? I sure hope so.

I made this decision myself when I was just a young boy. I was eight years old at the time. This decision has changed my life in so many ways.

It hasn't always been easy living with the consequences of this **most important decision**, but I wouldn't go back and change a thing about making it.

My life would have turned out a lot differently without making this decision. As a matter of fact, many of my other decisions since making the **most important decision** might have been different.

STARTING THE JOURNEY OF FAITH

By now I'm sure you're asking the very important question: "What is the **most important decision**?"

Well, I'm so glad you asked that.

Keep reading.

THE MOST IMPORTANT DECISION

Chapter 2
What is the Most
Important Decision?

Okay. I won't keep you in suspense any longer.

The **most important decision** is choosing to answer the call Jesus made to fishermen, tax collectors, prostitutes, and even a few religious people.

What is that call?

Jesus went to these folk, the fishermen, tax collectors, prostitutes, and religious folk and said, "Come, follow me."

When I was eight-years-old, a neighbor invited my sister and me to Vacation Bible School. In case you're not familiar with this concept, it was

THE MOST IMPORTANT DECISION

like a week or two of kids meeting at a church where they heard Bible stories, sang songs, drank juice, ate cookies, and made crafts.

I remember sitting in that church basement, with the cinder block walls, listening to a teacher share the story of a God who loved us so much he sent his only Son to die for our sins. He rose from the dead, we were told, and if we asked him to be our Lord and Savior, he would come into our lives and change us from the inside out.

Now I had never been to church before. I had never heard of the Bible or Jesus. I grew up in a secular Jewish home. This was all foreign to me.

But something happened to me. I didn't know it at the time, but looking back, I believe the Holy Spirit was touching my eight-year-old heart with a desire to follow Jesus.

The teacher asked us to pray something like this:

Dear Jesus,

I know that I'm a sinner. I believe Jesus died for my sins. I believe he rose from the dead.

STARTING THE JOURNEY OF FAITH

*Right now, I ask him to come
into my life and be my Lord
and Savior.*

*I will follow him the rest of
my life.*

*Thank you so much for
forgiving me and giving me
your gift of eternal life.*

Amen.

That July Monday in 1963, I became a follower of
Jesus. And I have been following him ever since.

I know this was the **most important decision** I
ever made.

As I already shared with you, it has had profound
and marvelous effects on my whole life.

Now, I've grown a lot since making this **most
important decision** in 1963. I've studied
theology. I learned to translate the Scriptures from
the original Hebrew and Greek. I can even find
the book of Haggai without using the table of
contents in the Bible!

THE MOST IMPORTANT DECISION

Now most of you might not be able to teach theology, translate Scripture, or find Haggai, but all of you can join me in making this **most important decision**.

I've had the joy of pointing hundreds of people to Jesus since someone pointed me in the right direction back in 1963.

Now you can wait until the end of the book—or right now—God might already be tugging at your heart and soul to make this **most important decision**.

You can borrow the prayer of an eight-year-old boy from 1963 and start that beautiful journey of faith right now.

Or…

You can keep reading and gather some more information.

Chapter 3
Why Do I have to Make this Most Important Decision?

This is an important question you probably have by now: **Why do I have to make this most important decision**?

Again thanks for asking another great question.

I have to start with a presupposition. You might not agree with it but this presupposition is foundational to everything else I share and to the world-view to which I adhere.

Here it is:

The Holy Bible is God's Word. He used men and women writing under the inspiration and illumination of the Holy Spirit. The Bible communicates to you and me God's special

19

revelation. It teaches us who he is. God's Word instructs us to know him and the life he has for us.

Paul told his young apprentice, Timothy…

> All Scripture is inspired by God and is useful to teach us what is true and to make us realize what is wrong in our lives. It corrects us when we are wrong and teaches us to do what is right. God uses it to prepare and equip his people to do every good work.
> 2 Timothy 3:16-17

So, with that foundation, I can share with you that the Bible teaches us that all of us are lost, all of us live in the darkness, all of us are born with enmity in our heart toward God, and all of us are sinners.

Sin is not a very popular word. When you and I think of sin we probably think of words like lying, stealing, murder, and wearing white after Labor Day!

But sin is very simply going our own way rather than God's way. Sin is like heading the wrong

way on a one-way street—you're bound for an
awful collision if you keep going in that direction.

Paul wrote his friends in Rome...

> ...everyone has sinned; we
> all fall short of God's
> glorious standard.
> Romans 3:23

Everyone. You, me, the saintliest person you
know, and the most horrific person you've ever
heard of—all of us have sinned—none of us can
measure up to God's holy standards.

"But I'm a pretty good person," you might be
thinking right now.

I'm sure you are. But being pretty good is not
good enough. Only God is completely holy,
righteous, and without one miniscule speck of sin.
And he cannot tolerate anything in his presence
that would compromise his holiness.

That's why Isaiah wrote,

> We are all infected and
> impure with sin. When we
> display our righteous deeds,

THE MOST IMPORTANT DECISION

> they are nothing
> but filthy rags.
> Isaiah 64:6

And that creates a problem for you and me. Well, it's a problem if you believe in life after death.

The Bible teaches that there are two final destinations after one takes his or her final breath on this planet—heaven or hell.

You might be asking, "Now, do you believe in streets of gold and sitting on clouds listening to harp music? Do you believe there's a place with fire and brimstone?"

Well, whether or not there are literal streets of gold or literal fire and brimstone (I'm not even sure what brimstone is), I don't know.

Here's what I do know.

Heaven is what the Bible teaches is living for eternity in the presence of God with joy, peace, and fulfillment.

Hell is living for eternity in the absence of God with suffering, sorrow, and loneliness.

STARTING THE JOURNEY OF FAITH

Again, I look to what Paul wrote to his friends in Rome…

> For the wages of sin is death, but the free gift of God is eternal life through Christ Jesus our Lord.
> Romans 6:23

You see, hell is really what Paul calls death—eternal death—not simply when our heart stops beating, when our blood stops circulating, and when our brain stops firing off electrical impulses. Eternal death is the absence of God. This is hell.

Paul says this eternal death is the wages of sin. In other words, we all deserve this. We all have earned this final destination.

But there's something else here. There's a gift. One does not earn a gift. One does not deserve a gift. A gift is given at the pleasure of a giver.

God is the divine Giver and he gives the gift of eternal life through Christ Jesus our Lord. This is heaven, and so much more.

THE MOST IMPORTANT DECISION

This is the meaning of the beautiful word **grace**. Grace is receiving a gift that one does not deserve or earn.

You and I, because we go our own way, deserve or have earned eternal punishment.

But God is a Giver—a gracious Giver. He delights in giving his precious gift to all who answer his call to follow him.

How does that sound to you so far?

Do you realize that you are lost? Do you realize that you are living in darkness? Do you realize that you are going the wrong way on a one-way street? Do you realize you are heading for a final destination that will not be a pleasant way to spend eternity?

I'm guessing by now you might have another question.

Chapter 4
How Do I Make this
Most Important Decision?

I was hoping you'd ask this question: **How do I make this most important decision?**

First of all, remember that your **most important decision** is based on God's call to you.

Whether you're mending your nets by your boat, like the fishermen Peter and Andrew, or sitting at your tax collector's booth like Levi, or like the prostitutes, or even the religious people Jesus met, it starts with him looking at you, saying, "Come, follow me."

Somehow, even as you're reading these words, you can "hear" in your heart those words. I don't mean you're necessarily hearing God audibly, but you are sensing his presence in your soul.

Like a kite hidden in the clouds, you can still feel his tug on your heart.

This journey of faith starts with him, not with you.

Listen to Paul's instruction to the Ephesian believers...

> Once you were dead because of your disobedience and your many sins. You used to live in sin, just like the rest of the world, obeying the devil—the commander of the powers in the unseen world. He is the spirit at work in the hearts of those who refuse to obey God. All of us used to live that way, following the passionate desires and inclinations of our sinful nature. By our very nature we were subject to God's anger, just like everyone else.
> Ephesians 2:1-3

STARTING THE JOURNEY OF FAITH

Do you understand what Paul is writing here?

He is telling all of us, you and me, that we are dead because of our sins. In other words, you and I are born *spiritually dead,* meaning we are separated from God.

You might have heard the story of Adam and Eve—the first two people God created. He put them in a beautiful garden. They were completely innocent. He only gave them one commandment: "Do not eat from the tree of knowledge."

But the devil, that wicked, slithering serpent came to them. He had them question whether God had their best interests at heart.

And after his hissing suggestion, they made the first wrong turn on the one-way street. They decided to go their way rather than God's way.

You and I have inherited this rebellious spirit. It's in our DNA.

That's what Paul meant when he wrote that all of us are dead because of our sins.

Remember, God told them that the day they disobeyed him they would surely die (see Genesis

THE MOST IMPORTANT DECISION

2:17). Well, they didn't die physically that day. They died spiritually. They lost their relationship with the God who created them.

You and I share the same spiritual disease with our ancient ancestors.

But Paul continues…

> But God is so rich in mercy, and he loved us so much, that even though we were dead because of our sins, he gave us life when he raised Christ from the dead. (It is only by God's grace that you have been saved!) For he raised us from the dead along with Christ and seated us with him in the heavenly realms because we are united with Christ Jesus.
> Ephesians 2:4-6

Wow! Did you catch it?

We deserve death because of our sin.

But God…

Those are two wonderful words, *But God…*

STARTING THE JOURNEY OF FAITH

But God is so rich in mercy. There we go again with that gracious gift we don't deserve. He loved us so much.

The penalty for sin and rebellion is a death penalty. That's what you and I deserve.

But God...

But God is rich in mercy. Jesus took off his robes of glory, clothed himself with human flesh (we theologians call this the incarnation), and died in our place.

But more than that, he rose from the dead. He bodily walked out of that grave three days later.

He is the one who is now tugging at your heart. He is the one who somehow you hear in your soul, whispering right now, "Come, follow me."

"How do I make that **most important decision**?" you ask.

You say, "Yes, Lord." I will follow you.

Paul told the Romans...

> If you openly declare that
> Jesus is Lord and believe in

> your heart that God raised
> him from the dead, you will
> be saved. For it is by
> believing in your heart that
> you are made right with God,
> and it is by openly declaring
> your faith that you are saved.
>   Romans 10:9-10

The Romans knew exactly what Paul meant here. In his day, people would be executed if they refused to say, "Caesar is Lord."

Paul is not just giving you and me "magic words" to say. He is letting us know that we need to declare absolute allegiance, not to a human emperor, but to the Creator of the Universe who desires a personal relationship with you and me.

That's what it means to *openly declare that Jesus is Lord.*

But there's more. The Christian life is a journey of faith. Faith is believing in something even when you can't see or explain it. Faith is absolute trust.

STARTING THE JOURNEY OF FAITH

When I get on a plane, I have faith. I don't understand how this metal tube weighing tons can carry me from Boston to Dallas.

Faith is trust.

When you become a follower of Jesus you are believing and trusting that Jesus died for your sins and rose from the dead.

You are trusting with your heart and declaring with your mouth that you will follow him all the days of your life.

Back to what Paul shared with the Ephesian believers...

After informing them that they were born spiritually dead; after giving them the good news that God is rich in mercy, he continues amplifying the gift of God's grace.

He tells them that God also raised them from the dead and seated them in the very presence of God.

You see, when God calls us to follow him, when we answer that call with a resounding **YES**, God makes us spiritually alive and brings us into his presence.

THE MOST IMPORTANT DECISION

In other words, you begin that journey of faith after you make that **most important decision**.

But please take note, this is a journey. Some of you might be putting off this **most important decision** because you see the inconsistencies of many of us who claim to be Christians.

Once we make this **most important decision** we start on the journey—we haven't reached the final destination—the presence of God yet.

Paul told the Corinthians…

> …anyone who belongs to Christ has become a new person. The old life is gone; a new life has begun!
> 2 Corinthians 5:17

Let me give you a better translation…

…anyone who belongs to Christ has become a new person. The old life is going; a new life is coming.

You see, I knew that Greek translation class would eventually come in handy.

STARTING THE JOURNEY OF FAITH

When you and I make this **most important decision** we are not immediately and instantaneously made perfect.

We start a journey—a journey of faith where day-by-day—with ups and downs—we become more like Jesus.

There is a day coming when we will be completely perfect.

John writes of that day…

> Dear friends, we are already God's children, but he has not yet shown us what we will be like when Christ appears. But we do know that we will be like him, for we will see him as he really is.
> 1 John 3:2

That's right. If you've been putting off becoming a follower of Jesus or checking out his church because those of us who are followers aren't perfect—no worries. We aren't. But one day, when we meet Jesus, we will be like him—holy and blameless.

THE MOST IMPORTANT DECISION

But those who neglect making this **most important decision** will have another future—a very unpleasant future.

So, before you make this **most important decision**, you realize that he made the decision first—to call you and say, "Follow me."

Our response is to say, "Yes, Lord."

God gives us another gift as we begin this journey of faith. What is this gift? Repentance.

Repentance literally means to change your way of thinking and your way of behaving.

The Apostle Paul commended the Thessalonians for their acceptance of this gift. He told them that people all over were talking about their faith:

> ...for they keep talking about the wonderful welcome you gave us and how you turned away from idols to serve the living and true God.
> 1 Thessalonians 1:9

The word translated *turned away* is the Greek word for repentance.

STARTING THE JOURNEY OF FAITH

Remember, we said a life without Jesus Christ is like going the wrong way on a one-way street. Repentance is turning around and going God's way.

By the way, when you make this **most important decision** and start going the right way on the one-way street heaven throws a party.

Yes, it's true. This is what Jesus said…

> …there is joy in the presence
> of God's angels when even
> one sinner repents.
> Luke 15:10

So, **how do I make this most important decision?**

1) Realize God has made the first move. He has called you to follow him.
2) Declare verbally that Jesus is the Lord or CEO of your life.
3) Trust him completely. After all, he conquered death and wants to lead you on that victorious path.
4) Allow him to help you change your direction. Go his way, the right way.

THE MOST IMPORTANT DECISION

"Now wait a minute. Don't push me too fast," you might be thinking.

"There are lots of other religions. There are lots of paths. Why should I make this **most important decision**? Isn't there another way?"

Wow! You ask great questions. Keep reading.

Chapter 5
Isn't There Another Way?

Don't all roads lead to God? After all there are all kinds of religions, faiths, cults, and spiritual paths, right?

Well, I suppose there are quite a few different roads people take. But here's where I have to go back to that presupposition I mentioned earlier.

Do you remember? I shared that I believe the Bible is God's Word.

Jesus said,

> I am the way, the truth, and the life. No one can come to the Father except through me.
> John 14:6

THE MOST IMPORTANT DECISION

That's pretty clear. Jesus said there's no way any of us can live in the presence of God without him.

Many people reject this simple plan and try and come up with their own plans or their own paths.

I don't know about you, but I'm going to follow the plan made by the Son of God who died in my place, rose from the dead, and offers me forgiveness, peace, and joy.

You see, when you make this **most important decision**, you are not climbing the road to heaven. That's religion.

I define religion as our attempt to reach God. But Christianity is not about our attempt to reach God. It is about God reaching down to us. God became one of us in the person of Jesus. Christianity is about him leading us on his path. He is the way. He is the truth. He is the life.

Some people think they're Christians because they go to church a few Sundays a year. I've heard it said that going to a garage won't make you a car. Going to a hospital won't make you a surgeon.

STARTING THE JOURNEY OF FAITH

I've also heard it said that religion is spelled, **"DO."** People think they have to do the right things. No, Christianity is spelled **"DONE."** A relationship with God is not about what you do but **what he has done** for you on the cross.

That's what the Apostle Paul was telling the Ephesians...

> God saved you by his grace when you believed. And you can't take credit for this; it is a gift from God. Salvation is not a reward for the good things we have done, so none of us can boast about it. For we are God's masterpiece. He has created us anew in Christ Jesus, so we can do the good things he planned for us long ago.
> Ephesians 2:8-10

"But this isn't fair. How can you say that Christianity is the only way to God?"

Well, first of all, I didn't say it. Jesus said that he was the only way.

THE MOST IMPORTANT DECISION

Men and women died for this belief. Before the followers of Jesus were called Christians they were called followers of the Way. That's how important this truth was and is.

Oh, you also said, "This isn't fair."

You're right. It isn't fair. Do you know what else isn't fair? That the sinless Son of God would take our filth and guilt on himself—the fact that he suffered our death penalty so that we can have eternal life.

I love the way the Apostle Paul put it…

> For God made Christ, who never sinned, to be the offering for our sin, so that we could be made right with God through Christ.
> 2 Corinthians 5:21

If you are going to make this **most important decision,** you will need to believe the one who calls you to follow him. You can go your own direction—remember it's the wrong way on a one-way street. I don't think you're going to like the way it ends.

STARTING THE JOURNEY OF FAITH

But there is only one way to the presence of God.

When Peter and John, shortly after the death, resurrection, and ascension of Jesus stood before the Jewish Supreme Court, they were commanded to stop teaching about the Way.

This is what Peter said to them,

> There is salvation in no one else! God has given no other name under heaven by which we must be saved.
> Acts 4:12

So, I guess it's time for me to ask you a question, Are you ready to make that **most important decision?**

THE MOST IMPORTANT DECISION

Chapter 6
The Decision

Well, now it's time for you to determine if you're ready to make this **most important decision**.

Do you feel God's tug on your heartstrings?

Are you ready to declare allegiance to Jesus as the Lord or CEO of your life?

Do you believe that he has risen from the dead?

Are you ready to answer, "Yes, Lord" to his invitation—"Come, follow me."?

Then, it's time.

THE MOST IMPORTANT DECISION

If you're ready to make this **most important decision** it means you're ready to ask the Lord to help you change your direction and go the right way on the one-way street of your journey of faith.

You will be done with trying to go it alone. You will experience the joy of forgiveness and fulfillment. You will not just have an eternal future in heaven. You will also have the most exciting journey of faith as you follow him and learn to live a life that pleases your Savior.

So here we go. It's decision time.

Do you remember that prayer I prayed when I was eight years old? Let me share that with you again.

> *Dear Jesus,*
>
> *I know that I'm a sinner. I believe Jesus died for my sins. I believe he rose from the dead.*
>
> *Right now, I ask him to come into my life and be my Lord and Savior.*
>
> *I will follow him the rest of my life.*

STARTING THE JOURNEY OF FAITH

Thank you so much for forgiving me and giving me your gift of eternal life.

Amen.

Do these words express your heart? The words we use aren't as important as the heart. God knows your heart.

The point is have you said, "Yes, Lord. I will follow you."?

If so, may I be the first person to welcome you into the family of God. And right now, all heaven is throwing a party for you! Pretty cool, right?

If you have a chance, would you email me and let me know you made this **most important decision**? Just email me at roger@rogerhaber.com. Thanks.

Alright, I bet you have another question.

What do I do now that I'm a follower of Jesus?

Another great question, I'm impressed.

THE MOST IMPORTANT DECISION

Chapter 7
What's Next?

Again, congratulations my new brother or sister in Christ. (Of course, if you were not ready to make that **most important decision** and are still reading, you can go back to that little prayer when you actually hear God calling you and feel his tug on your heart.)

"What do I do now?" you are wondering.

Well, let me give you a few suggestions.

First of all, why don't you tell someone about this **most important decision** you made. (You might want to even let them read this book so they might have that opportunity too.)

THE MOST IMPORTANT DECISION

Second, you need to learn more about Jesus whom you have committed to follow on your brand new journey of faith. I'd suggest you start reading the Gospel of John in the Bible. This book describes the life of Jesus and the life he has called you to live.

For example, one of the most memorized verses in the whole Bible is in this Gospel (Gospel by the way means *Good News*):

> For this is how God loved the world: He gave his one and only Son, so that everyone who believes in him will not perish but have eternal life.
> John 3:16

Third, I'd suggest you find a church that preaches the Good News. When you become a follower of Jesus—when you make this **most important decision**—you become part of a community of faith. You are not the only one on this journey.

Christianity is not a solo sport—it's a team sport.

Speak with the pastor. Share with him or her that you have begun a relationship with Jesus. Find out if there are opportunities for you to grow in your

STARTING THE JOURNEY OF FAITH

journey of faith. Find out how you can become part of this new community of faith.

If you're not sure how to find a church where you can continue that journey of faith, feel free to email me. Perhaps I can help you.

Fourth, remember you're in a spiritual war now. Yes, I need to tell you that. It's not easy being a follower of Jesus. There is an enemy of our Lord and his followers. He's the same serpent who came to a garden. He's the same foe who enabled our first parents, Adam and Eve, to doubt God.

The Apostle Paul told the Ephesians...

> Be strong in the Lord and in his mighty power. Put on all of God's armor so that you will be able to stand firm against all strategies of the devil. For we are not fighting against flesh-and-blood enemies, but against evil rulers and authorities of the unseen world, against mighty powers in this dark world, and against evil spirits in the heavenly places.

THE MOST IMPORTANT DECISION

> Therefore, put on every piece
> of God's armor so you will
> be able to resist the enemy in
> the time of evil. Then after
> the battle you will still be
> standing firm.
> Ephesians 6:10-13

You see, before you made that **most important decision** the devil wasn't going to bother you. After all, you weren't a threat to him.

But now you are a follower of Jesus. But you don't need to fear him. When you follow Jesus he is with you. He is more powerful than this wicked enemy.

But he will try and get you to doubt God. He will try and tell you that you're not good enough. He would love for you to go back to that one-way street—going the wrong direction.

But don't listen to him. He is a liar. He is a deceiver. He already knows he's defeated.

But as Paul told the Ephesians, he has armor available for you so that you can stand firm against all the wicked schemes of this evil enemy.

STARTING THE JOURNEY OF FAITH

That armor is the faith, righteousness, and salvation God has graciously given you.

And finally, you have the opportunity to come to God any time and talk with him. We call that prayer. It's not about fancy words filled with spatterings of "thees" and "thous."

You can actually talk to God like you talk to a friend.

You can start the day telling God how much you love him. You can thank him for his precious gifts. When you "drop the ball" (and you will, we all do) you can ask him to forgive you and help you change direction—back the right way on his one-way street.

Remember, when you make this **most important decision** you are on a journey—a journey of faith. If you're like most of us (alright, all of us), there will be times you'll stumble and fall. There will be times you'll be discouraged. There will be times when God might seem far away.

Don't worry, all of this is normal. Faith is trusting God even when he seems distant. Faith is trusting God even when you go through the darkest valley.

THE MOST IMPORTANT DECISION

Most of the great heroes of faith and in the history of the church have gone through some dark periods.

But we're on a journey. We're running a race. It's not a sprint—it's a marathon. It's going to take some time and you need to pace yourself.

Remember what the writer of Hebrews wrote...

> Therefore, since we are surrounded by such a huge crowd of witnesses to the life of faith, let us strip off every weight that slows us down, especially the sin that so easily trips us up. And let us run with endurance the race God has set before us. We do this by keeping our eyes on Jesus, the champion who initiates and perfects our faith.
>   Hebrews 12:1-2

You are in for the journey of a lifetime. You are in a race where the people who've gone before you are cheering you on.

STARTING THE JOURNEY OF FAITH

Keep following Jesus. Keep running the race. Don't let sin slow you down or trip you up. Get rid of it by asking Jesus for forgiveness every time you feel that stumble coming. And most importantly, keep your eyes on Jesus. He's standing at the finish line. Remember, he's already run the race. He's already experienced victory. And he's there, waiting for you to run into his loving arms.

You've made the **most important decision**. Now experience that journey of faith until you step into that joyful eternity God has prepared for you.

THE MOST IMPORTANT DECISION

About the Author

Born in the Bronx, NY, Dr. Roger D. Haber is a graduate of Stony Brook University and Gordon-Conwell Theological Seminary. He holds a Doctor of Ministry degree from Northern Baptist Theological Seminary.

Presently serving as Senior Pastor of the First Baptist Church in Randolph, Massachusetts, Dr. Haber began preaching at the age of 16. He has served as a pastor for over thirty-five years.

His previous books, *Christmas First Persons—Sharing the Story Creatively; Do All Dogs Go to Heaven?—Grieving the Loss of Your Pet; You Better Learn Baby Talk! You're a Grandparent* are also available on Amazon.

THE MOST IMPORTANT DECISION

Look for his upcoming books soon: *A Great Cloud of Witnesses—Listening to Faith Heroes; The Church as Orchestra—A Symphony of Praise to the Master Conductor; Praying as Jesus Prayed—Reflections on the Lord's Prayer; and Unwrapping God's Christmas Gift.*

Dr. Haber is married to Nanci. They have two adult sons (and one daughter-in-*love*), two grandsons, and one dog. They reside in Randolph, MA.

Dr. Haber can also be heard on his radio broadcast, **SearchLight** on WVBF 1530AM out of Taunton, MA. For more information
and to listen online, check out—

http://www.hometowntalkradio.com.